# What If It Were You?

# What If It Were You?

A Collection of Human Rights Poetry

## Elizabeth Arif-Fear

SHEPHEARD-WALWYN (PUBLISHERS) LTD

First published in 2019 by
Shepheard-Walwyn (Publishers) Ltd
107 Parkway House, Sheen Lane,
London SW14 8LS
www.shepheard-walwyn.co.uk

British Library Cataloguing in Publication Data
A catalogue record of this book
is available from the British Library

ISBN: 978-0-85683-526-1

Typeset by Alacrity, Chesterfield, Sandford, Somerset
Printed and bound in the United Kingdom
by 4edge Ltd

*Dedicated to my late mother*
*– the strongest, most selfless person to have*
*blessed my life and to whom I owe so much.*
*You remain forever in my heart.*

*This collection is also written in solidarity*
*with all of the men, women and children across*
*the globe who have been victims of injustice.*
*You have a voice. You are not forgotten.*
*These are your stories.*

# Acknowledgments

Sincere thanks go to my family and friends for their continued support and encouragement. Thank you for everything that you do!

A big thank you goes especially to my friends Rachel, Doreen and Saima, and my dear husband for their advice, assistance and support – in particular with the translations and transliterations in this work. Thank you!

Lastly, but above all, *alhamdulillah* for His continuous blessings, which have enabled me to become the person I am today and to write this book.

## Trigger warning

The content of this book focusses on a range of sensitive issues, many of which readers may find distressing.

A listing of support services can be found at the back of this book to enable those affected to seek advice and support and for all readers to be able to find out further information about the issues raised and how you can help.

# Contents

# Foreword

*What If It Were You?* is a book meant to stir the very basal emotions within us that link us to others. It talks to the humanity within us all and attempts to unravel the tentacles of both civil injustice and harmful cultural norms which strangulate and otherise both individuals and whole communities or sets of people. Written by a human rights activist within Muslim and secular communities, the book speaks a truth that is much needed as an antidote to the cultural and social manipulation of basic human rights norms which should instead have been placed at the fundamental heart of many countries.

Arif-Fear speaks about the sickening realities of child marriage, female genital mutilation and modern slavery and picks up on issues that are affecting many, many lives across the globe and in the UK. She highlights the plight of refugees, the infamous and inhumane 'Jungle' where young men and women's lives remain wasted away in Calais and the war in Syria which has decimated the historical, cultural and human capital of the country. She is fearless in her drive to expose the socio-cultural norms that have been imposed on people and the injustices which many men, women and children continue to face worldwide.

Speaking to Muslim, secular and non-Muslim communities, Arif-Fear seeks to burst open the chains that hold mindsets down so that patriarchy and abuse within communities and civil societies can be challenged. She looks for bridges of understanding, whilst challenging the barriers of ignorance and intolerance.

Some of the very people that Arif-Fear challenges are those men who have been born into privilege just because they are males. Speaking for women and minorities, she is countering the extremist and misogynistic narratives of men placed at the helm of women's lives. It is this passion for life, for humanity and for human rights, that makes Arif-Fear someone to watch in the future. She is shaping a path that many women still fear to tread – challenging faith leaders, holding them to account and bursting open the mental prisons they have created to hold down women and minorities, whilst also challenging wider structures of power, hierarchy and injustice.

Arif-Fear is blazing a trail driven by her faith, based on a human rights approach. This book is testament to her values, her ideals and her beliefs. It also places her at the vanguard of challenging practices that have damaged lives, emotions and minds. If there is anything we can be sure of, it's that this book will set the scene for her work in the future.

FIYAZ MUGHAL OBE

# What If It Were You?

As the sun rises,
As the new day awakens,
There's no morning cheer,
No blissful glowing sky,
No bright new day of life, hope and possibility.
No, as the sun rises,
So do the bombs,
The shells,
And the bullets.

As the sun rises,
So do the screams and the heartbroken cries
Of a mother whose baby lies lifeless in her arms,
Of the orphaned child whose hopes and dreams are
    snatched away so cruelly in a single second,
Of a husband whose heart has been twisted, crushed
    and shattered into a million pieces…

No, no blissful glowing sky,
No hopes,
No dreams,
No possibilities,
No cheer.

Instead, there lies a bloody cursed battlefield
Where the streets cry out with waves of blood,
Where the walls crumble with sorrow and fear,
Where the earth knows nothing but death and
    destruction.

No, instead here lies a blazing battlefield a million
    miles away...
A million miles away from your shores,
A million miles away from your doorstep,
A million miles away from you.

But what if it were you?
What if it were your mother,
Your child,
Your soul,
Your heart,
Your everything?
*What if it were you?*

What if it wasn't them,
What if it wasn't "the other",
The "stranger",
The "foreigner"?
No...
*What if it were you...?*

# I Am a Woman

I am a woman.
I'm equal in worth – or so they state,
Equal in dignity and rights – though late.

But am I equal as you shut me from view?
When your voice so loudly silences the few?
When you cut my flesh to safeguard desire?
When your position is always, always higher?

Am I equal when it's books I can't reach?
And isolation that you so fondly teach?
When the choice to cover is not mine but yours?
When my body's your source of open doors?

…

I am a woman.
I'm equal in worth – that is true,
Equal in dignity and rights as you.

But when I can simply just be me,
Then – and only then – will I be the woman you
    don't see.

*Dedicated to Azza Soliman*

# Cut

She was young and hopeful,
Building a dream –
A dream for a future she had not yet seen.

She was just a child,
Merely twelve years old,
Simply doing the things she was lovingly told.

She would never imagine,
As she flew to this land,
The pain, the torment and the red-stained sand.

Drip,
Drip,
Drip.

Now the rusty blade was ripping her flesh,
With tear after tear,
Her soul left so bare...

It cut away her freedom
And that which was dear,
Because of the values that they do so fear.

Drip,

4

Drip,
Drip.

They cut away her choices,
Her future and pleasure,
Emancipation? Equality? No, never!

Drip, drip,
Gone.
Forever.

She was young and hopeful,
Yet scared to dream,
For there was so much of life she should never
    have seen.

She was just a child,
Merely 12 years old,
Yet for the price of "honour",
Her flesh had been sold.

# Your Guilty Secret

The right to free speech, belief and to life,
These are the freedoms which cause you such
    strife.
Yet the more you aim to oppress and pry,
The louder our calls for justice will cry.

For we,
We know your guilty secret...

We know how you ruthlessly silence their voices,
And violently erase such crucial life choices.
We know how you bar them from their families
    and homes,
As for you, they're simply mere flesh and bones.

For we,
We know your guilty secret...

Yes we know how you violate their rights and
    humanity,
With such utter unimaginable brutal barbarity.
We know how you cut from beneath their own
    skin,
Stealing live living organs for monetary win.

For we,
We know your guilty secret...

So although you may try to hide physical proof,
We'll keep on fighting to share the truth.
For *we* will not let you escape without trial,
Whilst the charred blazing bodies form an
     invisible pile.

We call on the world to shout out your name,
Yes, the Falun Gong are your real true shame.
We know your guilty secret and humanity will too,
Because rights are for all – not merely the few.

# Covered

Layers of silk, of cotton and twine,
All in service of The Divine.
Wrapped snug and tightly, I feel close to Him,
The One against whom I so often sin.

The softness of the cotton cap against my skin,
Is part of me and my soul – it's not a whim.
It's the way I live, learn and truly feel,
It's my crucial decision to choose to conceal.

I cover my hair, my neck and head,
And not because I have merely been wed.
I shroud my arms, my legs and my chest
In garments of love and obedience as part of my
    test.
The test of devotion, of love and patience – not
    strife.
No, not a prison of iron-fisted might.

I cover for Him and no one else,
This is me, my body, my soul and self.
The choice is mine alone and never yours,
So do not feel you need to "save me from the Lord".
No, I do not need my head laid bare,
Nor do I need you to stand and stare.

Neither do I wish to hear their cries,
Their criticism or their lies.
Brothers in faith they may be,
But equality is not what I see.

# Free

I am free,
Free like the howling wind,
Free as I raise my voice and shout out loud at the
    injustices I see –
Both the good and the bad.
For I have a voice,
For I am free.

My life may not be a picture of aesthetic perfection,
Of jewels, shimmering gold and all that glistens,
But my life is one of truth, justice and reality –
The reality of strife, determination and endeavour,
The reality of freedom.

I am free and nothing is dearer than being able to
    taste the rich soothing aroma of my heart as it
    sings out loud
And pours out its sweet melodious beauty of truth.
No, nothing is more beautiful than the rush of
    release in your veins,
When you tear away from the rusty bloodied chains
    of man.
No, nothing except the soothing touch of Allah Almighty
    encapsulating your heart and soul.

Dear brothers and sisters,
I see you as you walk our streets with your bags and
    treasures in hand,
And I stop and think: I would never wish away my
    life for yours –
For one of luxury and seemingly vivid dreams…
For the real price of your Riyal is one of freedom,
Imprisoned in a golden palace of four glistening
    walls,
Draped in swathes of silk,
And bathed in soft sweet musk.
Your uniform is the luxury designer fashion of many
    a dream,
Your life one of such apparent ease.
Yet a life of freedom is real, honest and true,
For a life of freedom is truly and utterly priceless.

# Double Standards

They say heaven lies at the feet of your mother,[1]
To love your wife and simply no other.
Yet they deny their daughter the right to choose,
And thrust upon her a list of "don't"s and "do"s.

They express how our beloved Prophet (peace be
    upon him) honoured the women in his life,
Yet the misogyny and sexism is shockingly rife.
Yes, they tear away at her beautiful skin,
And sell her as a prize for men to win.
They deny her the right to seek knowledge and
    truth,
Cutting short her precious, innocent youth.

For they do not wish for her to seek pencils and
    books,
But instead live a life to clean, birth and cook.
Instead, she is merely a vessel, a body and a slave,
Born to serve the interpretation that man has so
    ignorantly made.

---

1 *"Fal zamuhaa fa'inna al-Jannata taht rijleyha"* (Prophet Muhammad (pbuh),
    al-Nasa'i)

But no, oh no, my God is one of truth,
One of light, love and intellectual proof.
So woe to the men of fear and shame,
Who cause such unbearable suffering and pain!
You may live your life freely at will,
But I will not lie down, silent and still.
For I will shout out the truth and all that is *ahsan*,[2]
In the name of Allah, The Merciful, Al-Rahman.[3]

2 Pure and good (i.e. not corrupted) (Arabic)
3 The Most Merciful (Arabic)

# Family Reunion

A brother you've never met,
A sister you don't greet –
For these are the sacred family,
Of whom we never speak.

We share the same forefather,
Of one blossoming family tree,
And so many similar habits –
If only you could see.

They love our single God,
No partners to Him aside,
But ashamed to unite together,
We stand apart with pride.

They call to the sacred land,
A land of peace unknown.
Here too we used to bow in thanks,
In worship to Him alone.

The prodigal brother and sister,
Estranged in daily life.
Yes, this has been a family,
Who've faced such utter strife.

*Barukh Atah Adonai,*
*Rabb al-'Alameen,*
*Poke'akh ivrim,*
*Ihdina as-Sirat al-Mustaqeem.*[4]

4  "Blessed are you, Lord" (Hebrew)
   "Lord of The Worlds" (Arabic)
   "Who opens the eyes of the blind" (Hebrew)
   "Guide us to The Straight Path" (Arabic)
   (Pokeach Ivrim, Morning Blessings, The Koren Sacks Weekday
   Siddur (Jewish), Surah al-Fatihah (Qur'an, 1:2,5) (Muslim))

# Dry Wounds

Dry wounds,
The markings of a pain that's never seeped violent,
    flowing red,
For these are instead the wrinkled wounds from the
    words he often said.
Invisible to world around; the naked, attentive outer eye,
But sadly still present after many a year has passed by.

Dry wounds,
The remnants of a story – so very real yet with no trace
    upon your skin,
For these are the remains of a battle you never
    understood you were in.
Now simply the eternal scabs left upon your soul, mind
    and heart,
They're faded in age yet never fully healed – despite the
    fresh start.

Dry wounds,
The imprints left by the grazing, burning words of a man
    in fear,
From the sounds echoed when it were your voice he
    couldn't hear.
The shrill of the drunken command: "Pick up the phone
    bitch!"

Telling you it was *your* time to leave and your friends to
    quickly ditch.

Scars,
The answers to those unexpected, paranoid, cutting
    questions,
Of doubt and guilt with oh so such absurd suggestions!
The demands of *when*, *what* and *if* anything had
    happened with him,
Asking outright if you'd crossed moral barriers – yes,
    how very grim…

Scars,
The sore remains of the feelings you both shared in his
    confused strange way,
No, it was never, ever enough to ever, ever stay.
Ultimately, the final dagger would cut too deep into
    flesh too bare and raw,
As he eventually slurred: "So you're one of *those* girls" –
    yes, this was the final straw.

Scars,
The everlasting reminder of what's now supposedly
    passed, healed and simply gone,
But the hurt never truly ends – not when the dagger's so
    painfully long.
Yes, these are wounds which still lie within your soul –
    now embedded upon your heart,
Even though you chose to save yourself, for you would
    *not* be torn apart.

Dry wounds,
Scars,
The shrivelled drops of poison dried upon your soul –
The reminders of the lessons which forever you will hold.
For these are no longer the fresh signs of abusive
     heartbreak,
But instead a reminder to love yourself – for your own
     true sake.

# Strength

Protection…
                Oppression.

Modesty…
                Shame.

Honour…
                Imprisonment.

Duty…
                Pain.

Weakness…
                Strength.

Love…
                Abuse…

*Lies*…
                *Truth*.

# Fear

Fear is the closet that seals hearts shut
To the love that others cannot understand,
Forcing many an innocent person to follow the "law
of the land".

Fear is the invisible veil of women,
Who dare not speak out at the injustice they feel,
Because *honour*, *shame* and *ignorance* are all too
very real.

Fear is the silence of men, women and children,
Sold in chains of sex, labour and daily pain,
All for easy simple monetary gain.

Fear is the solitude of a single man,
Alone and silent in his cell,
Slowly dying in a blackened hell.

Fear is the panic of a woman who sees her baby fall
into the waves of the cold hard sea,
With millions of others hoping to flee.

Fear is the blood trickling down her legs,
As she's "cleansed" pure, ready to be wed,
All so her family know she'll be fed.

Fear is silence,
Fear is pain.
Fear is taboo,
And fear is shame.
Fear is the devil himself,
Fashioned by the chains of men,
Who tell society *how*, *what*, *who* and *when*.

# Why Do You Hate Me?

Why do you hate me?
Am I not your sister?
Your mother?
Your brother?

Do I not bleed the same colour as you?
Does the same rusty red not rush through my veins?
Does my heart not beat to that same steady thump,
    du-dump, du-dump?
Do I not breathe the same sweet air as you?
Cry like you?
Smile like you?
And hurt like you?

Why do you hate me?
Am I not your sister?
Your mother?
Your brother?

Do we not worship the same God?
Do we not both cry out in pain in our darkest hour?
Longing for His soothing touch,
To heal our souls,
Wipe away our tears,
And make us whole again?

Why do you hate me?
I am simply your sister,
Your mother,
Your brother.

I am simply a Muslim,
Not an "other".

# Fragile

Women…
Women are fragile he tells me.

Fragile…

Delicate, fragile and weak,
Like a blossom in a blushing, subtle shade of pink,
Gently swaying in the wind, so soft and sweet,
Who will always fall so gracefully at their feet.

Women…
Women are precious he tells me.

Precious…

Precious, beautiful and rare,
Like a sparkling pearl in its shell, so divine,
With a beauty so dazzling and glowingly fair,
She *must* be concealed and to men never ever left
    bare.

Women…
Women are difficult he tells me.

Difficult…

Difficult, unpredictable – an enigma of the mind,
Like the glowing desert and the burning sand,
She is a tease who turns innocent men blind,
Through her mirage, illusions and fashioning of time.

Women…
Well I say:
I am not a delicate blossom, a precious hidden pearl
    or the burning hot sand.

I am a rose.
A rose so brightly red like the burning passion of fire,
A rose so vibrant like the strength of my beating heart
    rising higher and higher.

I am a rose.
A rose with thorns, strong, prickly and sharp,
Ready to rip the flesh of *any* men who threaten to tear
    my soul apart.

No, I am not fragile, precious or difficult to read,
I am a woman of strength – not a womb for your seed.

So take heed and do not seek to conceal me, silence
    me or dampen my spirit,
For I am not a mere vessel of your imaginary inner
    limit.

# Home

She longed for a place to call her own,
For life in a tent was simply no home.

Close to her heart was a dear land she was forced to
    flee,
A war-torn haven her soul cried so often to see.
Now she longed for a warm bed and somewhere safe to
    play,
As she'd grown so weary, day after day!

Each night she'd close her eyes and to God she'd pray,
To see her mother and father alive in the blissful shining
    day,
To silence the screams she'd heard on the bloodied
    streets of hell,
For there was raw deep sadness of which she'd never
    tell.

No, she no longer wished to relive the feel of the waves
    battering against her skin,
On that nightmarish journey – the battle of life which
    many wouldn't win.
Yes, she'd reached the sands, yet she yearned to silence
    the cries engrained in the sinking rubber,
And find herself instead in the arms of her dear, sweet,
    gentle mother.

Instead, she dreamed of being back where her heart
    belonged,
With her parents and siblings who'd been so sorely
    wronged.
She yearned to be shrouded in love and nestled in a
    deep comforting embrace,
With a home-cooked meal and a familiar smiling face.

Alas, if only she were able to open her eyes and find
    she was no longer alone.
If only she could simply just be home...

# Just Like You

They tell her she's wrong,
That she's "unnatural"
And unsound...
But is it unsound to feel?
To love?
To hurt?
And to live?
Just like you?

For her heart beats,
Her spirit rises,
Her eyes cry,
And her soul stirs,
Just like you.

Her heart skips a beat when she sees her smiling face,
Her spirit rises when she hears her melodious voice,
Her eyes cry hot streaming tears as they long to look
    once again into hers,
And her soul longs to meet her twin once again.
For she feels, she longs, she loves, she hurts and she
    lives,
Just like you.

So yes – they may share the same organs,
And the same genetic code,

Yet theirs is a love that no human can deny the other –
A candle that nobody can extinguish,
A yearning that stirs so deep inside her soul that no
    one can tell her she is "wrong" –
For she is merely like me and you,
Simply, and utterly *just like you*.

# Hope

My name is Ali,
And I am a prisoner of misfortune,
An inmate of hell,
A soldier of justice,
Found at the wrong time,
In the wrong place,
And in the wrong life,
Tried and charged for that which I never committed.

Now I live in a dark, damp squalor of filth and
    deprivation,
Where my bed is the cold hard floor of injustice,
My food the sustenance of misery,
And my friends the companions of my mind.

For in the full darkness of day, follows the deep
    depths of night,
And as I lie here with no one other than my soul to
    accompany me,
I stare at the night sky as black as the spirit that lies
    within me.

And as I stare, I am joined by a handful of speckled
    sparking lights,
Beaming under the cold night sky.

Each one reminds me of the dark long years I have
    spent in this cell –
A prison of pain, solitude and lifelessness,
Devoid of light, joy and freedom.

Yet I must go on – I *will* go on,
For a battle without end is a battle already lost.
I will *not* let them take my soul,
For they have already taken my life, my home, my
    heart and my body.
Yes, I *will* carry on,
I *must* carry on.
For as long as I can see those shiny sparkling lights,
I know that there is hope,
I know that the world stands with me,
And I know that there is indeed justice in this world.

My name is Ali,
And I am a prisoner of misfortune,
An inmate of hell,
And a soldier of justice.


*Dedicated to Ali Aarrass*

# What Do You See?

*What do you see when you look at me?*

Do you see a doctor, a lawyer, a teacher or nurse?
Or a cook, a maid and a life-long curse?

Do you see school books, shopping trips and carefree
    evenings with friends?
Or entrapment in the same four walls through one
    singular lens?

*What do you see when you look into my eyes?*

Do you see joy and happiness for the future ahead?
Or fear and panic of bleeding red?

Do you see excitement, contentment and peace of
    mind?
Or a struggle for answers I will never find?

*What do you see when you look at the gold around
    my neck?*

Do you see luxury, love and safety from harm?
Or chains of misery, dependence and alarm?

Do you see sparkling jewels of celebration and joy?
Or a price paid to be his virgin toy?

*What do you see when you look at my white dress and
    diamond ring?*

Do you see a future of tenderness, compassion and love?
Or pain, torture and cries of mercy to The One above?

A *bride* is what they tell me they see,
Yet I am a just a girl, born to be free!
For *I* am merely 14 years old,
A child eager to learn – not to be sold.

Yet, when they look at me, they see a future, pride and a
    life without shame,
Yet my heart feels such sorrow, sadness and pain.
From *this* I gain nothing except fear and sorrow,
From *this* I am denied the right to my own true
    tomorrow.

Why do they not see me for the girl I am,
And bear witness to my innocence and pain?
Do they not see my streaming hot tears falling like rain?

My heart is instead broken,
My soul is screaming out in fear.
Oh how I wish I could simply not be here…
Yet alas my childhood lies shattered into a million pieces,
For the reality of today never truly ceases…

# Empty Streets

These are the empty streets where women know no
    name nor place,
Out of sight and mind – devoid of any real true
    space.

For their "own protection" and reputation,
Their domain remains the four walls of their home,
To shield them from the men who fear women alone.

They fear their very voice, their footsteps and their
    subtle gaze,
They doubt their beauty, their freedom, their minds
    and soul,
And instead enforce upon them one single life goal.

Designed by the self-proclaimed "stronger sex",
Theirs is the role of silence, obedience and sin,
In a battle many women do not push to win.
Yet what these men do not declare is that the hatred
    they hold,
Is simply their self-loathing and insecurity left untold.

For women a place they simply *cannot find*,
So as the streets lie empty and the women adorn the
    home,

Around the village the men eagerly roam.
Alas, they carry on according to their single superior
    vision,
For to not be seen as whores, these women must
    remain hidden.

# Coconut

I'm not brown,
I'm not white,
I'm me.
Is colour all that you see?

I stand up against hate,
And you state that I'm against race,
People of colour and faith.
Do you not see me, brother?
My brother from another mother?
Is the pattern of my scarf invisible to your eye?
Do I not strive and try?
I'm just trying to figure out why!
Why, you'd abuse a sister in faith,
Simply because she stands up against hate?

You see, I'm not a hater,
Nor a racist
Or a player.
I'm not a fruit, a dessert, a pudding or naysayer.
I pity how you try to silence me with
A mere colour code of fools.
It's people like you
Who can't accept what's true!

You see brother,
I'm not brown,
I'm not white,
I'm me.
Is colour all that you see?

I'm a Muslim,
Just like you.
But why does that not ring true?
You see your soul is charred by the hatred of fools.
They're using you brother, like a tool!
They don't care if you're black, white, brown or blue,
What they care about is silencing the few –
The few who stand up against hate,
Who won't accept such a shameful fate,
The few whose vocabulary is not simply to rate:
One, two and three –
*Thaub*, *kufi*, *sajaadah*[5] in hand – check!
Never mind justice, truth, obeying the laws of the
    land…

And you call *me* a coconut?
"Brown" on the outside and on the inside "white"?
No brother.
I'm not brown,
I'm not white,
I'm me.

5 Prayer gown, cap and rug (Arabic)

Is colour all that you see?

It's such a shame brother that you're so colour blind –
Blind to the colourful purity of hearts and minds.
Is this what you think Prophet Muhammad (peace be
    upon him) stood for?
Division, hatred, simply bowing on the floor?
For when you bow to Allah Almighty, you bow in grace –
Not in hate.

Brother – open your soul, your mind, your ears,
Stop spreading such simple fears!

You see, it's easier to love than to hate,
So step back brother – before it's too late…

# I Am Not Human

I am not human,
I'm a piece of meat.
I'm sexual pleasure,
Lying at your feet.

I'm a liver, a kidney,
An organ or two,
Living and breathing,
So you can too.

I'm a labourer,
Washing your car,
Cleaning your kitchen,
Working at your local nail bar.

I am not human.

I'm an object with a price tag,
With chains around my neck –
Chains you do not see,
But that follow me, me, me…

I am not human.
I have no choice,
No voice.

For I am not human.

# Hypocrisy Is Spelt with a Y

He wants nothing other than a virgin bride,
But thinks nothing of spreading *himself* far and wide.

He wants a woman to earn and work,
But also to cook, clean and birth.

He seeks abundant pleasure inside the marital bed,
But never seeks to satisfy the women he wed.

He instead seeks the night to meet, mingle and often
    greet,
Whilst his wife feels the same four walls beneath her
    feet.

Yes, he too demands his sister's suitor be a prince
    amongst men,
Whilst with his wife, it's *he* who dictates *how*, *why* and
    *when*.

Yes, he demands respect, affection and truth through-
    out,
Whilst he dictates, screams and so mightily shouts.

For he seeks double standards – one for him, another for
    you,

A formula of ages that remains ever true.
It's double X for you and a Y for the oh so mighty and
    high,
Yes, it's hypocrisy and it's spelt with a "Y".

# Idol of Oppression

*"Bi ruh, bi dam, nafdik ya za'im!"*
*"Bi ruh, bi dam, nafdik ya za'im!"*
"My leader, I sacrifice my soul and blood for you!"

How they shout out your name,
Jeering in praise for a man who simply has no
    shame.

They raise up their blood-stained hands,
Soaked with the cries of the innocent engrained in
    the lands,
Buried deep in the blazoned soil as a witness to the
    injustice and inhumanity,
Cursed as their soul rises to give account of the utter
    barbarity –
The barbarity of men who call you a hero...

*"Bi ruh, bi dam, nafdik ya za'im!"*
*"Bi ruh, bi dam, nafdik ya za'im!"*

But I never knew a hero whose level of mercy was
    absolutely zero,
A hero who kills, murders and gasses the young...
Tell me again how you're a hero left unsung?

Yet still your "men" continue to shout out your
    name,
Like cloned clowns of everlasting pain:

*"Bi ruh, bi dam, nafdik ya za'im!"*
*"Bi ruh, bi dam, nafdik ya za'im!"*

Yes, *this* is a pain they inflict even on the nation's
    dear youth...

No, do not tell me there is no proof,
For I have witnessed the torture with my own eyes
    and ears,
Through photos, accounts, and oh the many, many
    tears!
A beast of humanity is what I see...
Yet how can it be that a father, a husband and a son
    could stoop so low?
And turn millions of innocents into such a foe?

Lo! You are their idol, like a god of devils.
They call out to you from the lowest of levels –
A level of humanity beyond mere man,
As they murder the innocent because of oppression
    they're simply *no fan*.

*"Bi ruh, bi dam, nafdik ya za'im!"*
*"Bi ruh, bi dam, nafdik ya za'im!"*

Indeed, no cry can be louder than that of the
    haunted souls innocently slain,

Mound after mound of bodies left lain.
For they are the idol worshipping sheep –
An idol of evil, the soulless and weak.

They surely have sold their souls for the love of an
    oppressor,
Paid though the blood of those they deem "the
    lesser".

*"Bi ruh, bi dam, nafdik ya za'im!"*
*"Bi ruh, bi dam, nafdik ya za'im!"*

Behold, the land is calling out for mercy and a shred
    of truth,
As you continue to deny the unimaginable proof.
Yet the world is watching and waiting dear *za'im*.

Alas, they may think: never, not him!
But every idol does indeed fall,
No matter how inhumanly tall…

# Binaries

Black, white.
Gay, straight.
Right, wrong.

Is it really that simple?

Male, female.
Young, old.
Believer, non-believer.
Cis, trans.

Is it really that simple?

Is it really as simple as our minds
    would lead us to believe?

Us, them.
You, me,
Never born to be free –
Free to be who we are,
How we feel,
And how we wish to live?

No, I am me.
You are you.
And *we are free.*

# Two-Faced Feminist

He calls you his equal, worthy of love, life and respect,
Destined for a life of integrity and success.
His equal pure and simple, intended to reside in peace,
For which the violence and conflict should finally cease.

Yet this is the rose-tinted façade he proudly displays,
To capture his woman, his bride, his maid.
Dare you look a little further, you'll see there's many a
    truth to hide,
Behind the rose-coloured mask of mountainous lies.

For when a brother spreads his loins and choses freely
    where to lie,
His comrades jeer with him in praise so loftily and high.
Yet when a woman is violated and her flesh burnt by the
    hands of might,
*She* is the blameworthy, clothed in nakedness, "shame"
    and the inability to fight.

For when the mask slips, the real face of lies, false
    promises and truth is laid bare,
And slowly the darkness of his soul is no longer so rosy
    and fair.
Instead, as the wedding is over and your dress of purity,
    hope and innocence falls to the floor,

You're left bare and, willing or not, his property – for
your dreams are no more.

He now calls you his wife, his princess, the queen of the
home,
For this is the place where you shall forever now roam.
Day after day, the world will be out of sight – for his
demands are all you shall hear,
And to go against his wishes is a fate you'd never dare fear.

Instead, the certificate on the wall you so wilfully gained
through sweat, blood and tears –
Yes, the fruit of your independence, your mind, your very
soul and strength,
Has become nothing more than an ornament of the past
hung high at length.
Adorning the walls of his palace, your potential is lost,
For what has become a burdensomely *heavy, heavy cost*.

For here you shall live in a myriad of apparent love,
obedience and joy,
For you are his queen, his wife, his beloved toy.
Yet this is instead a "love" where each lover knows their
limits, their role, their place –
A love that mirrors his unashamedly two-sided face.

For he called you *"his equal"*, worthy of love, life and respect,
Yet the reality of these two words remain un-checked.
For him, a feminist he can never be –
He's a two-faced misogynist – if only the world could
see…

# Blind Hearts

*Blindness*
When you're trapped in the blackened depths of your
    soul's inner desire,
Engulfed in the raging flames of yourself, rising higher
    and higher.
Where the cooling streams of peace are parched dry
    and left crumbling and bare,
As to think for the needs of others, you never would
    dare.

*Blindness*
When you see not the beauty of light and truth,
And instead reject all rational proof,
For the windows of your soul shut out every ray of
    light,
Out of ignorance, fear and childish fright.

*Blindness*
When the bitterness of hatred runs through your
    veins,
Your blood mixed with that of many a man so sorely
    pained.
When your heart beats to the echo of judgement and
    sin,
As every good deed counts for simple self-win.

*Blindness*

When your heart is starved of mercy and wisdom,
For those not officially "of His Kingdom".
When you're deaf to the piercing cries beneath the
    barrier of division,
As the reality of the wider world to you remains hidden.

*Blindness*

When you see life as *halal* and *haram*, good, bad, black
    and white,
Colour blind to the hues, the tones and realities of life.
For indeed, the reality is that *it's not their eyes that are
    blind,*
But in fact *their hearts, souls and very minds.*[6]

---

6 "Fa'innahaa la ta'ama al-abasaaru wa lakin ta'ama al-qulubu al'lati fii al-sudur" (Qur'an, 22:46)

# Invisible

Invisible are the padded shapes curled into the
    darkened corners of our streets,
The minds and hearts we refuse to seek.
The lonely, the cold, the hurt and torn,
The restless, the sombre, the ever forlorn.

Invisible are the shadows wrapped in a tatty sleeping
    bag,
Wishing to be noticed as a real person – not simply
    sad.
Instead drenched in hail, sleet and freezing rain,
They live a life of faded hope, torment and pain.

For invisible is the woman who's fled the tightening
    hands around her neck,
A man who's home life was nothing more than a
    harrowing wreck.
A worker left out in the cold with nothing left for a
    rainy day,
A friend who's run out of options for rent he cannot
    pay.

Yes, these are the invisible minds and hearts we refuse
    to seek,
For invisible to our eyes is never the bottle at their feet.

Instead, by this single object we choose to judge as we
    see,
Yet this is their companion to drown the sorrows that
    may sadly be.

Alas, invisible to our minds, hearts, eyes and ears,
Are their sorrow, their pain, their doubts, their fears.
Their stories remain untold as we continue to judge
    others for a life we do not know,
As we carry on, seeing others by simply everything on
    show.

Yet these invisible souls, hearts and people are lying on
    our streets across *our* land,
Crying out for a loving ear, a shoulder to cry on and a
    helping hand.
Yet we walk past them day by day and deny their place,
For invisible they remain – forever subjected to hate.

# Warriors of Barbarity

The "warriors of piety and truth" – or so they say,
They raise up their guns believing *this* is the way.
They bow to our loving God – one of wisdom and
   truth,
Yet outside in the streets, of Him there is simply *no
   proof*.


For in their "nation", there is no shred of kindness,
   mercy or simple free will,
No, nothing except the desire to enslave, maim and
   savagely kill.
Indeed, in their self-declared precious "State of God,
   truth and faith",
There is nothing but fear, loathing and despicable
   hate.


Yes, here on the streets lie the bloodied traces of men
   and women who can no longer be,
Who can no longer worship their God(s) in peace and
   tranquillity – nor simply be free.
Alas, these streets know not love, nor peace, nor a
   common humanity,
No, nothing except such utter militant, savage
   barbarity.

Once gone is the innocent laughter of children and
women – who now remain a shadow of whom they
once were,
As the blackened reality of daily life has become such a
misty blur.
For instead of laughter, smiles, love and peace,
Lies a cloud of darkness which may never cease.

Yes, here in "their land" of blood, death and pain,
Lie the bodies of every "dissident", homosexual and
innocent slain.
For as you walk amongst the streets, hung up high
are the severed heads, limbs and souls of "the
unworthy", "the infidel" –
Those whom they so self-assuredly claim are "going
to hell".

Alas! Their way is nought but a path of violence, guns
and flowing blood,
Where the streets lie amassed in a barbarous flood.
For what they fail to so crucially see,
Is that they call for nothing but a sexual, violent killing
spree.

No, they call not for God, for His Prophet or for
anything holy,
They call for *barbarity*, *inhumanity* and all that is lowly.
Yes, what they fail to understand is that the hell they
so greatly fear,
Is already so sadly, clearly here.

For no matter how loudly they cry the name of God
the Most High,
They call to the devil inside – not the sacred sky.
For when they lift up their guns, their knives and their
chains of lust,
They harden their hearts of stone – their organs now
dust.
For true believers they are not, nor "men of God" or
Allah,
They are merely men and women who have strayed
instead so very, very far.
No, they are not "warriors" of peace and justice or
the message of oneness and clarity,
No, these are instead the forsaken souls – the
"warriors" of barbarity.

# Steps of Hate

Hijab:
    Muslim,
        woman,
            oppressed…
Kippa:
    Male,
        Jewish,
            Jew…
Turban:
    Asian,
        foreign,
            Taliban…
Mini-skirt:
    short,
        sexual,
            loose…

Person:
    *Individual, human, being.*

# Angel beneath the Ground

A beacon of love, hope and joy,
She was merely a seed – not yet a girl or boy.
A precious gift of mercy and shining light,
How could she ever have known of her upcoming fight?

Instead, this little gift grew and blossomed amongst the
    beating soul of her mother so dear,
In a cocoon of warmth and love with never a thought of
    fear.
Yet, day after day, and with the passing of each new
    night,
She also moved closer and closer towards the eternal
    light.

For as the days, weeks and months passed by,
So too drew nearer her mother's cry.
And as her mother's screams of pain eventually called
    out loud,
The new parents waited anxiously to become ever so
    proud.

Yet as the screams grew louder and louder and the truth
    drew near,
The cocoon of love and comfort instead transformed
    into fear.

For as the shining light above her legs grew brighter and
     the blessing of life was born,
The truth was revealed and the parents were torn.
Revealed in bare, blunt truth was the fear of
     disappointment, poverty and shame,
For which this little one would never ever be blessed
     with a name.

Alas, sadly the reality of the life so small, warm and true,
Was just too much for a family with money so few.
Having so quickly entered into the burning light of day,
In the eternal light, this little one would now find her
     way.
For this joyous blessing would return to the light after a
     passage of darkness and pain,
Torn away from those who would never have treated her
     brother the same.

For a toddler, a child, an adult she would never be,
Only in another world could she ever be free.
Yes, never would she be cherished, welcomed nor even
     found,
For instead, she was now an angel beneath the ground.

# Ya Suriya! (Oh Syria!)

*Ya Suriya!*
My heart bleeds for the pain and anger you endure year
after year,
Yet every tear I shed, *ya Suriya*, is merely a drop in the
countless seas you cross in search of security and
home, free from the pain, conflict and fear.

*Ya Suriya!*
The pain I feel is real but nothing more than a single
fresh cut into the deep-seated bloodied wounds of
your soul,
Torn apart by war and bloodshed, *ya Suriya*, as down
the barrel bombs roll, roll, roll…

*Ya Suriya!*
I see your tears, your screams of pain and the anguish
burning deep within –
I feel helpless, *ya Suriya* – a mere bystander, a witness,
a muted voice ashamed of the sin.

*Ya Suriya!*
Your land lies in tatters of rubble and stone,
Yet please never ever forget, *ya Suriya*, that you have a
home.

*Ya Suriya!*
Humanity stands with you,
Our hearts bleed and for *you*, will never ever cease.
*Ya Suriya!* We will never ever give up –
Never ever, until you find peace.

# Shattering the Glass

*My target is clear*,
Clear and transparent as the light of day –
It's my reminder of the men in black, white and grey.

It's the window through which all females see,
Just how easy for men it can be.

Yes, it's the film that weighs down heavy above my
    head,
A burden-laid ceiling which I'll tear into shreds.

*My target is pre-destined*,
From birth, to graduation – when I receive my paper in
    hand,
Even here in the "freest of lands".

It's the rule that I can read the same books and study
    the same degree,
Yet it will all be a greater struggle to become financially
    free.

Yes, it's the law that when you toil with equal measure,
    you'll get lower pay,
And instead be left striving and striving for another way.

*My target is unjust*,
For suited and booted, they glide up the mountainous
    prism of testosterone and masculinity,
Whilst I push through the layers of crystal and glass
    defined by femininity.

But no – I'll shatter the glass into a million pieces,
Into jewels of red, yellow, purple and blue,
Into a prism of hope for everyone – not simply the few.

My target is *me*.

Yes, I'll shatter this horrid ceiling as I am striving for life –
A life of equality and equity – for I am not simply a wife.

I'm a woman, a warrior and possessor of strength,
And I'm already shattering the glass at a single arm's
    length.

# My Prophet

I often wonder what my beloved Prophet (peace be
    upon him) would say,
If he were to come back for just one day,
Into a world of conflict, chaos and war –
A world that always wants *more*, *more*, *more*.


I often wonder if he were to witness the depravity to
    which we continue to sink,
What would he really, truly, honestly think?
What would he say to the brother who mistreats his
    dear mother?
To the one who claims to speak for himself, his wife and
    each and every other?


How would he feel to learn of the dogma entrenched in
    his faith,
And witness such bitterness and unimaginable hate?


What would he think, feel and even say?
Well, he'd fall to his knees and to Allah Almighty he'd
    pray!
He'd pray to save the souls of his very own kind,
Against the bitterness of our hearts and poisoned
    minds.

Indeed, how would he feel to see his *Ummah*[7] in a
   spiritual sleep?
Well, my Prophet would simply stand and weep.
For we know not God, His message or His unimaginable
   love,
Alas, we know not The One above.

7  Nation (i.e. global Muslim community) (Arabic)

# Inhuman

As the screams grow louder and louder with every cell
of their being,
He slyly carries on without a single thought for their
feeling.
As the cries for mercy beg for a shred of peace and an
end to the insufferable pain,
Their words become mere shadowy whispers echoed in
vain.

For at his feet lie the bodies of innocent souls so cruelly
battered, bruised, bloodied and torn,
Whilst "the protector" shouts, threatens and berates to
so cruelly "warn".
From out of his mouth flow the poisonous words of lies,
torture, torment and pain,
From a vessel that is no longer human – for inhuman
is his name.

*Inhuman…*

Inhuman is his heart, hands, words and the smile
engraved so brazenly on his lips –
A smile of pleasure as his victims lie shattered from their
broken skull to their fractured hips.
Inhuman is the laughter as they cry so deeply for an
ending, a release, for mercy and peace,

Whilst he drags them along the floor like animals left to
   beg at his feet.

*Inhuman…*

Inhuman is the man who burns, electrocutes and defiles
   the inner flesh of not just women but men too,
Tearing their body from the inside out in ways you could
   not imagine were true.
Inhuman is the torture of innocent people who dare to
   speak out loud,
Inhuman is the man of whom evil he is *so, so proud*.

*Inhuman…*

Inhuman is he who seeks pleasure from the raw savage
   pain of others,
The source of heartbreak of bereaved parents, families
   and traumatised mothers.
Inhuman is the one who leaves his victims to
   "disappear" without a single trace.
Inhuman yes, for these are the despicable specimens of
   the so-called human race.

# Not You

I see your words,
I see your name,
I see your letters,
But I don't see You.

I see your books,
Your Creation,
Your miracles,
But I don't see You.

Inside their four walls,
Of the mind and soul,
I see people,
I see words,
I see promises,
But I don't see You.

I see not your mercy,
Your kindness,
Your love,
Your justice,
Your perfection.
No, I don't see You.

For such beauty is invisible to the minds of hatred,
Of intolerance and sin.
Such beauty is instead "weakness",
Deemed "unlawful",
And "blasphemy".

Instead, I see everything that You stand against,
Everything that You call out,
Everything that You are not.

I see sorrow,
Confusion,
Hatred,
Intolerance,
And bigotry.
Yes, *this* is what I see.
For what I do not see is *You*.

# Honour

*Honour*
It's the rule of my life – my principle, my guiding truth,
It's the rule for which I need no rational proof.
With honour my wife, my sister, my daughter are all
    mine,
And so they must *never ever* cross the line.

*Honour*
It's my pride, my crown, my glory, my every being,
It's my ears and eyes awake, alive and all-seeing.
Honour is my coat of arrogance as I walk the open
    streets,
Displaying my feathers of purple and teal, stomping
    my feet.

Honour is the entangled web spun with the opinions
    of others – what they'll think and say,
And no, it can never ever be any other way –
For they'll start to talk and the hushed whispers will
    follow,
And the tainted murmurings will forever dictate our
    tomorrow.
No, I *cannot* have my reputation bruised and my man-
    hood shrunk –
Honour is my right – just look how low those whores
    have sunk!

For honour, our name cannot be tarnished in filth and
    shame,
Dirtied by free will and desire – as they so often claim.
So do not ask me for an answer – it's just the way it is
    and forever will be –
It's our culture, our traditions – she *can't* be free.
It's honour and it's not hers – it's *mine*, and only, *mine*.
So no – she must *never ever* cross this line.


...


*Honour*
It's the ongoing punishment that each and every day
    I live,
My burden, my prison – devoid of free will.
It's the huge black shadow that follows me wherever
    I go,
Telling me, yelling at me: *"No, no, no!"*


*Honour*
It's the chains around my neck and the shackles around
    my feet,
Dictating *who*, *when*, *why* and *how* I can and can't
    meet.
It's the words of control, rule and regulation,
Which dominate my home, my streets and very nation –
The dictionary of "bitch", "whore", "slut" and slag",
Where *they* dictate what's "good" and "bad".


For this is the poisonous vile they spit out as I try and
    seek my own life and truth,

The raw hatred and fear they exhume as I walk,
    ignoring their "proof".
For whereas I seek knowledge, education and
    professional pride,
They cannot bear for me to reject the man they force
    by my side.
Yet honour contains *my rights*, *my freedoms*, *my life*
    – belonging to *me* and no one else,
So roll away your poisonous tongue and reflect – the
    problem is yourself!
For you spit on the honour of me and my sisters
    worldwide,
Injecting your bitter venomous bile of insecurity and
    pride.

Yes, it is instead *you* who fears the manhood between
    the legs of every man,
As your inner most desires and anxieties cause you to
    curse, hate and ban.
But *no*, we are not walking wombs, mere sex on legs,
    "irrational" and "weak" –
No, we *cannot* be the validation you so sorely seek.

*Honour*
Your honour is poison, bitterness and hatred – the
    food of fools!
Well I will cling on with my life to my real honour
    – pure and true.
The rights I possess are *mine* not *yours* –
Oh how I pity your morality and education so poor!

So, whilst you shrivel away in your cave of bitterness,
    disappointment and pride,
I will live my life freely with my honour, my rights and
    *self-love* by my side.

# Undesirable Muslim

"Uncovered", head laid bare,
"Willing" and "wanting" the men to stare.


Too open-minded, too progressive, too small in number
    to be true,
Of Islamic practices they apparently "know too few".


A lover of their brother or sister, the same as their very
    self,
*They* instead say they're bringing in "innovation",
    "corruption" and need much help.


"No!" they cry – a believer who seeks the guidance of
    another man,
If he's alive and living, one simply "*cannot* be a fan"!


…


"*Khalas!*"[8] they declare – they *must* fit *our* form, *our*
    very shape and designated place,
Never mind if they call to despise one another or to
    spread poisonous hate.


8 "Enough!" (i.e. stop) (Arabic)

Alas, in *their* eyes, a woman, a man, a believer in truth
they cannot be,
For they think they have all the answers – if only they
could see!
For instead of diversity, discovery and inclusivity for one
another and the world around,
An *"undesirable Muslim"* is the label they're given,
that's so often found…

# The Jungle Never Dies

They call it "The Jungle",
Like the wild green natural lands where the animals
    roam,
Except this is not like any jungle I've ever known.

This is a jungle where instead of the roar of nature's
    beasts,
You'll hear the tearful cries of innocent children lying
    at your feet.
A jungle where instead of the green fruitful trees
    beaming high,
You'll see burned out wooden shacks and smoke-filled
    skies.
Yes, a jungle where instead of the peaceful sounds of
    singing birds,
You'll bear witness to the men in uniform's unwanted
    words.

You see, they call it "The Jungle",
But this is not a natural bounty of peace – a land of
    exotic animals and plants,
This is the refuge of innocent humans looking for a
    chance.
It's a crowded, unsafe haven for people as
    worthy as you and me –
Not a land of mysteries for all to see.

Yes, they call it "The Jungle" but less than a year on,
The site's been demolished and everyone's saying it's
gone.
But the reality is that The Jungle still exists,
For these brothers and sisters are still pushed to persist.
Yes, the fleeing are still stranded and left *alone* in this
foreign land,
In need of any kind of human helping hand.

Yes – The Jungle still exists and we're passing it by,
While young men looking for hope are crossing to die.
For those very tents and shacks may have been torn
down and thrown away,
But you can't throw away a problem – it's real and it's
here to stay.

# Weapon of War

Men in uniform, "rebels of the State" – the
    difference simply matters not,
Because when it comes to war, this is a weapon
    they've all shown they've got.
Yes, a weapon of deeper pain than you could ever
    imagine yourself,
A pain of spirit, heart, mind, soul and self.
For this is not a weapon of bullets, nor shells, nor
    singular blades or knives,
Instead, this is a weapon which seeks *mental and
physical genocide*.

Yes, this is a weapon of many an age – a weapon
    which has never really ceased to exist,
For indeed when war erupts, it's never far off in the
    dark blackened mist.
Yes, this is a weapon of flesh and power which stands
    against the very essence of mankind –
A weapon that in every "battlefield" you'll always,
    always find.
For with their rancid flesh of hell, they tear apart her
    heart, her soul, her every being,
Often forcing her loved ones to lie standing,
    witnessing and forever seeing.

Yes, with this weapon of hell, these soldiers leave
    many in fear and such stigma that many never tell,
Yet with some dear victims, their truth is out as their
    tummy starts to swell.
For with every thrust they push to destroy the
    humanity of every innocent women they find,
To rob, shame and torture minds as they batter, beat
    and grind.

Yet this is not a battle of mere sexual pleasure and
    gratification,
No, it's a battle of power, genocide and humiliation.
For when they seek to impregnate her innocent
    womb,
They seek to "water down her identity" and place it
    in a tomb.
Yes, they wish to remove every trace of her identity
    with such stark bare profanity,
And into the world bring their own "dear race"
    through an act of utter barbarity.

For theirs is a weapon of war like no other –
It's weapon against sisters, brothers, fathers and
    mothers.
No, it's not a weapon of bullets, nor shells, nor
    singular blades or knives designed to merely tear
    human flesh apart –
It's a *weapon of men* enacted to trample upon her
    *very own dear heart*.

# #MeToo

They call it "making love" or sometimes "having fun",
But *love* isn't taking a woman who's scared to run.
*Fun* isn't tearing at another person's hair, body and soul,
Taking them to a place of hell as their dignity you stole.

For she did not consent whilst she laid in another world
    with her eyes wide shut,
She didn't say: "Oh how I want you!" when she laid
    there cut.
Yet nothing could extinguish your selfish raging fire so
    cravenly stirred,
For your desires came first and her screams of silence
    remained unheard.

Instead, to you she was nothing but a body, a corpse, a
    piece of flesh,
Which you ravaged till her heart and soul met death.
For there could never be an interaction of hearts, minds
    or two people as one,
As there was no duality or shared desire – yes for her
    there were *simply none*.

Do you know how it kills her inside to hear your
    blameless words and talk of "shame"?
When shame is of an animal who steals without mercy,
    consideration or a second thought for pain?

Oh the shame of pulling away at her skin, her limbs and
    everything you so blindly sought,
Turning humanity into a throw away doll simply free to
    be bought!

Yes, it crushes her heart to hear your utter contempt for
    her freedom, her choices and her God-given free will,
Knowing you drowned out all conscience, reason and
    morality for a cheap violent thrill.
For you – yes *you* – couldn't look into her sleeping eyes,
    nor laugh or joke –
Instead in a sexual rage you were merely there to tear,
    pull and poke.

So what if she'd had a drink and with yourself shared a
    kiss?
What she didn't consent to was *ever, ever this*.
Yes, dear *"sir"*, lying together is not a battle of human
    might and power,
It's a meeting of equal souls, minds and flesh in their
    most intimate hour.

For you cannot deny how your sobriety towered over
    the one you failed to protect,
The one whose confidence – like her body – lies
    battered, bruised and wrecked.
For you knew she was vulnerable and needed a friend
    – not a sexual predator who'd instead take the lot,
Yet without a second thought – a look into her soul,
    heart and eyes – you decided to take, take, take and
    *that's what you got.*

You see, she didn't undress in act of sensual will – *you*
    ripped open her clothes,
Nor did she laugh – it was *your* ego which screamed and
    so loudly moaned.
No, she didn't lie with you – *you* alone towered heavily
    over her innocent self.
She was *your* sexual slave, owned so sorely by your
    selfish self.

For in that room, overcast was a blackened cloud of
    disregard and hate,
Hatred for a woman whom you'd trapped as bait.
For a body laying still, asleep and from reality so far,
Became your toy and ever immortal scar.

Yes, you knew with every cell of your being what you
    were doing and enjoyed every second of her burning
    pain,
As for you, none of it was ever, ever taken in vain.
Yet a year on it's *her* that has to live with the pain,
    violation and apparent blame,
For having acted like a so-called "dirty woman" of sexual
    "shame".

Yes, it's *her* life that has merged into a nightmare of
    "shame", pain and blackened heartbreak,
Whilst *you* instead continue to roam the streets as a
    blameless man – how fake!
Now, it's *her* that has to live with the life you so bla-
    tantly, ruthlessly and violently stole,

From the night you forced *your sober body* into *her dormant, innocent soul.*

Now, day after day she breathes the shattered reality
    which onto her you forever thrust,
But carry on she will, she can, she wants to, she must!
For whatever lies you continue to concoct and ruthlessly
    seek,
Know this truly and clearly: she didn't ask to be violated
    in her sleep.
For this is the truth – that is without question or room
    for doubt,
And with all her strength, she will always, always
    continue to shout.
For the reality is black, white, raw, real and ever true,
The victim is *her* – not you – and there's many others
    crying out loudly "*#MeToo*!"

Yes, take note: there are no greys, no blurry colours
    – there's no hazy middle ground,
It may be bleak but *you're* guilty and that's what the
    powers that be should have found.
Alas, for all the women and men whose sweet dreams
    you've ripped apart and turned into a living
    blackened hell,
Know that they're still coming out with the truth you
    thought they'd *never ever tell.*

# Kafir

*Allahu akbar, la ilaha ill Allah!*[9]
He calls out to God Most High,
Stretching out his hands towards the infinite sky.
Cleansing his body, his soul and his heart,
He prepares to lovingly, devotedly start.

*Allahu akbar, la ilaha ill Allah!*
He kneels to his Creator in serenity with grace to pray,
Just as he does each and every single day.
Yes, he reads from the same holy book and calls for the
    same prayer,
Yet, for anyone to call him a Muslim is ever so rare.

*"Kafir"* they call him.
"Disbeliever"!
"Blasphemer"!
Outside of their holy faith.
So much so, even this man's *life* isn't safe.

*Allahu akbar, la ilaha ill Allah!*
He reaches out to the needy, the infirm and old,
He helps the longing orphan child and those outside his
    fold.

9  "God is The Greatest, there is no god except [the One] God [Allah]!" (Arabic)

Yet because he follows a man living and anew,
He remains outcast by all around except a mere few.

*Allahu akbar, la ilaha ill Allah!*
Yes, he tests his thirst, his hunger and his desires too,
Just as you, me and many others also do.
Yet because of his beliefs, to the holy cities he has never
    been,
And is instead forced to watch the rituals through a
    television screen.

"*Kafir*" they call him.
"Disbeliever"!
"Blasphemer"!
Outside of their holy faith.
So much so, even this man's *life* isn't safe.

Instead, back home his mosque lies burnt and his books
    defaced,
With him and his family subjected to hate.
For from his lips must never fall the greeting of peace,
Or his future and life may lawfully cease.
For he is a "*kafir*" they say – not a Muslim brother,
Yes, he's an Ahmadi Muslim – an unwanted "other".

# What Is Freedom?

*What is freedom?*
Freedom is when I can speak the language of my soul,
When words of love, mercy and peace never remain
    untold.
When I can sing the melody of my soul till my heart is
    content,
And not find myself alone in a cell to repent.

*What is freedom?*
Freedom is a place where I can hold my beloved's hand,
And not fear the law of the ruling land.
When I know not the cold dampness of a prison cell,
For I'm never ever told I'm going to hell.

*What is freedom?*
Freedom is the feeling of home, of security and peace,
Where justice is everyone's right to seek.
Where the words of courts stem not from pain,
Nor from the mouths of men innocently slain.

Freedom is my right and it's yours too –
Where no one dictates *when*, *why*, *how* and *who*.

Freedom is a world where you and I are both equal to
    be,

Where we are finally free to live the dreams we see.
Where fear we know not and torture we never feel,
For freedom is the right of everything living and real.

# Further support and information

If you've been affected by any of the issues in this book or would like more information on how you can help those affected, please see the list of services and organisations below:

*Global human rights issues:*
Amnesty International
https://www.amnesty.org/en/

*Reporting crime:*
Crimestoppers
https://crimestoppers-uk.org/

**Specific services:**

*Anti-Muslim hate crime:*
Tell MAMA
https://tellmamauk.org/

*Anti-Semitic hate crime:*
Community Security Trust
https://cst.org.uk/

*Child protection:*
Childline
https://www.childline.org.uk/

NSPCC
https://www.nspcc.org.uk/

*Domestic violence and sexual assault:*

National Domestic Violence Helpline
http://www.nationaldomesticviolencehelpline.org.uk/

Rape Crisis
https://rapecrisis.org.uk/

Refuge
https://www.refuge.org.uk/

Survivors UK (male rape and sexual abuse)
https://www.survivorsuk.org/

The Survivors Trust
http://thesurvivorstrust.org/

Victim Support
https://www.victimsupport.org.uk/

Women's Aid
https://www.womensaid.org.uk/

*FGM support services:*

Forward
https://forwarduk.org.uk/

NHS
https://www.nhs.uk/conditions/female-genital-mutilation-fgm/

*Forced marriage:*

Forced Marriage Unit
https://www.gov.uk/guidance/forced-marriage#forced-marriage-unit

*Genocide:*

Holocaust Memorial Day Trust
https://www.hmd.org.uk/

Remembering Srebrenica
https://www.srebrenica.org.uk/

*Homelessness:*
Crisis
https://www.crisis.org.uk/

*Jewish-Muslim relations:*
Muslims Against Anti-Semitism (MAAS)
http://muslimsagainstantisemitism.org/

Nisa-Nashim
https://www.nisanashim.org/

*LGBTQI+ support:*
Hidayah (Muslim)
https://www.hidayahlgbt.co.uk/

Imaan (Muslim)
https://imaanlondon.wordpress.com/

Keshet (Jewish)
https://www.keshetuk.org/

Stonewall
http://www.stonewall.org.uk/

*Modern slavery:*
Modern Slavery Helpline
https://www.modernslaveryhelpline.org/

*Refugee and asylum-seeker support:*
Help Refugees
https://helprefugees.org/

Refugee Action
https://www.refugee-action.org.uk/

Refugee Council
https://www.refugeecouncil.org.uk/

*Victims of torture:*
Freedom from Torture
https://www.freedomfromtorture.org/

# About the author

ELIZABETH ARIF-FEAR is a writer and human rights campaigner based in London.

Passionate about human rights and interfaith relations, she founded the online platform Voice of Salam in 2015 to inform others about a range of human rights, interfaith, social and cultural issues and provide campaigning advice.

As an active writer, campaigner and organiser for a variety of human rights and interfaith bodies working on a range of issues such as modern slavery and interfaith cohesion, Elizabeth finds poetry to be one of the most powerful, expressive tools of writing to enable her to exemplify the injustice men, women and children encounter on a daily basis across the globe. Tackling a range of areas including FGM, child marriage, misogyny within the Muslim community, LGBTQI rights, Islamophobia and the struggles of refugees, religious minorities and war-torn communities, she uses poetry to raise awareness of the struggles fought by many – including herself – and to call for peace, justice and humanity across the globe.